First World War
and Army of Occupation
War Diary
France, Belgium and Germany

60 DIVISION
179 Infantry Brigade
London Regiment
2/16 Battalion
30 September 1915 - 30 November 1916

WO95/3030/6

The Naval & Military Press Ltd
www.nmarchive.com
Published in association with The National Archives

Published by

The Naval & Military Press Ltd

Unit 10 Ridgewood Industrial Park,

Uckfield, East Sussex,

TN22 5QE England

Tel: +44 (0) 1825 749494

www.naval-military-press.com

www.nmarchive.com

This diary has been reprinted in facsimile from the original. Any imperfections are inevitably reproduced and the quality may fall short of modern type and cartographic standards.

© **Crown Copyright**
Images reproduced by permission of The National Archives, London, England, 2015.

Contents

Document type	Place/Title	Date From	Date To
Heading	WO95/3030/6		
Heading	60th Division 179th Infy Bde 2-16th Bn London Regt. 1915 Sept 1916 Nov		
War Diary	Saffron Walden	30/09/1915	19/10/1915
War Diary	Bishops Stortford	26/10/1915	30/11/1915
Heading	War Diary Of 2/6th Battalion, London Regiment, from 1st December,1915 To 31st December 1915 Volume		
War Diary	Bishops Stortford	01/12/1915	31/12/1915
War Diary	Longbridge Deverill	01/02/1916	29/02/1916
Heading	DAG 3rd Echelon Here With War Diary For The Month Of June 1916		
War Diary	Warminster	14/06/1916	29/06/1916
War Diary	Neuville St Vast Area	30/06/1916	30/06/1916
Miscellaneous	Appendix I Strength.	21/06/1916	21/06/1916
Miscellaneous	Appendix II Casualties Return.	24/06/1916	24/06/1916
Heading	War Diary Of 2/6 Lond R. (Queens Westminster Rifles) July 1916 Volume II		
War Diary	Neuvilly St Vaast Area	12/07/1916	19/07/1916
War Diary	Bray	20/07/1916	27/07/1916
War Diary		01/07/1916	31/07/1916
War Diary	Neuville St Vaast Area	01/08/1916	19/10/1916
War Diary	Bray	20/08/1916	25/08/1916
Miscellaneous	2/16th London Regiment (Queen's Westminster Rifles)	01/09/1916	01/09/1916
Heading	War Diary Of 2/16th Battalion London Regt. (Queens Westminster Rifles). September 1st To 30th 1916 Volume IX		
War Diary	Neuville St Vaast Area	01/09/1918	12/09/1918
War Diary	Bray	13/09/1918	18/09/1918
War Diary	Neuville St Vaast Area	19/09/1918	30/09/1918
Miscellaneous	2/16 Lond. R. On 23.09.16.	23/09/1916	23/09/1916
Miscellaneous	Statement By Officers And N.C.O	24/09/1916	24/09/1916
Miscellaneous	Appendix III G.O.C. XVIIth Corps.	24/09/1916	24/09/1916
Miscellaneous	Extract From Battn Routine Orders	25/09/1916	25/09/1916
Miscellaneous	Extract From Divisional Routine Orders		
Operation(al) Order(s)	Report On Raid Carried Out In Accordance With My Operation Orders No.20	21/09/1916	21/09/1916
Miscellaneous	The Following Code will Be Used By Capt Flower		
Miscellaneous			
Operation(al) Order(s)	Operation Orders No.20 by Lieut-Colonel C.A. Gordon-Clark Comdg 2/16th London Regiment (Q.W.R.)	21/09/1916	21/09/1916
Map	Map		
Miscellaneous	2/16th Battn: London Regiment (queens Westminster Rifles)	01/10/1916	01/10/1916
Heading	War Diary Of 2/16th Batt London Regiment From 1st October 1916 To 31st October 1916		
War Diary	Neuville St Vaast Area	01/10/1916	06/10/1916
War Diary	Bray	07/10/1916	12/10/1916
War Diary	Neuville St Vaast Area	13/10/1916	24/10/1916
War Diary	Bray	25/10/1916	25/10/1916
War Diary	Tilloy-Hermaville	26/10/1916	26/10/1916

War Diary	Sibbeville	27/10/1916	28/10/1916
War Diary	Villers L'Hopital	29/10/1916	29/10/1916
War Diary	Ribeaucourt & Domesmont	30/10/1916	31/10/1916
Miscellaneous	Appendix III H.Q. 60th Div.	20/10/1916	20/10/1916
Miscellaneous	2/16th Battn London Regt (Queen's Westminster Rifles)	02/10/1916	02/10/1916
Heading	2/16 Battn. London Regt (Queen's Westminster Rifles) November 1st To 30th 1916 Volume XII		
War Diary	Ribeaucourt & Domesmont	01/11/1916	03/11/1916
War Diary	Bellancourt	04/11/1916	15/11/1916
War Diary	En Route For Marseilles	16/11/1916	19/11/1916
War Diary	At Sea	20/11/1916	21/11/1916
War Diary	Malta	22/11/1916	27/11/1916
War Diary	At Sea	28/11/1916	29/11/1916
War Diary	Salonika	30/11/1916	30/11/1916
Miscellaneous	2/16 Battn London Regt. (Queen Westminster Rifles)	01/11/1916	01/11/1916
Heading	60 Division 179 Inf Brigade 2/16 London Regt (Queens Westminster Rifles) 1915 Sep-1916 Feb		
Heading	60 Division 179 Inf Brigade 2/16 London Regt (Queens Westminster Rifles)		

WO 95/3030/6

60TH DIVISION
179TH INFY BDE

2-16TH BN LONDON REGT.

~~JLY - NOV 1916~~

1915 SEP - ~~1916~~

~~1916 JUN~~ - 1916 NOV

(MISSING 1916 MAR APR + MAY)

Confidential

WAR DIARY of A. 2/6th Londoners Army Form C. 2118.

Sept 1915

INTELLIGENCE SUMMARY.

(Erase heading not required.)

Hour, Date, Place	Summary of Events and Information	Remarks and references to Appendices
SAFFRON WALDEN 30.9.15.	Training was carried on during the month and the battalion was completed with all mobilization equipment with the exception of Machine Guns. Tactical work in Brigade on war scale was carried out.	copy
	7 men were discharged to commissions in the Territorial Force and new armies	copy
		As London Armd Road Cy 2/16th London Regt.

CONFIDENTIAL

Army Form C. 2118.

WAR DIARY of O.C. 2/16th London Regt
or
INTELLIGENCE SUMMARY. October 1915.

(Erase heading not required.)

Instructions regarding War Diaries and Intelligence Summaries are contained in F. S. Regs., Part II. and the Staff Manual respectively. Title pages will be prepared in manuscript.

Hour, Date, Place	Summary of Events and Information	Remarks and references to Appendices
SAFFRON WALDEN.		
5-10-15.	The Bn took part in a four days tactical exercise with 60th London Divn with full war equipment except machineguns	cyr
14-10-15.	The Bn took part in a two days tactical exercise with 60th London Division. (Trench warfare)	cyr
19-10-15.	The Bn took part in a four days tactical exercise with IIIrd Army	cyr
	The Bn moved by route march into billets at	cyr
BISHOPS STORTFORD 26-10-15.	BISHOPS STORTFORD.	
	4 NCO and men were discharged to commissions in the New Army and Territorial Force	cyr

A Gordon Clark Major
O.C. 2/16th London Regt
(Queens Westminster Rifles).

CONFIDENTIAL.

Army Form C. 2118.

WAR DIARY of 2/16th London Regt
November 1915.

INTELLIGENCE SUMMARY.
(Erase heading not required.)

Instructions regarding War Diaries and Intelligence Summaries are contained in F.S. Regs., Part II. and the Staff Manual respectively. Title pages will be prepared in manuscript.

Hour, Date, Place	Summary of Events and Information	Remarks and references to Appendices
BISHOPS STORTFORD 1-11-15. to 30-11-15.	The Battalion is billets in STORTFORD continued training of Machine Gunners, Signallers, Bombers, Scouts, Snipers & Stretcher bearers, and the training of officers and other ranks. On Nov. 13th '303 Rifles were issued to the men of the battalion and '256 rifles were called in. 5 men were discharged to commissions in the New Armies + Territorial Force	(sgd) (sgd) (sgd) W. Sudderland Col Cy 2/16 London Regt Queen Victoria's Rifles.

(73989) W4141—463. 400,000. 9/14. H.&J.Ltd. Forms/C. 2118/10.

C O N F I D E N T I A L.

War Diary of

the 2/16th Battalion, London Regiment,

from 1st December, 1915 to 31st December, 1915.

Volume

Confidential

Army Form C. 2118.

WAR DIARY
INTELLIGENCE SUMMARY
(Erase heading not required.)

O.C. 2/16 London Regt.

Hour, Date, Place	Summary of Events and Information	Remarks and references to Appendices
BISHOPS STORTFORD. 1.12.15.	Coy Training	cyr
2.12.15	Ceremonial	cyr
3.12.15	Annual Inspection by OC 179th Infy Bde	cyr
4.12.15	Foot Root & Kit Inspection. 1 man disch'd to Commission	cyr
5.12.15	Church Parade. 1 man disch'd to Commission	cyr
6.12.15	Bn on Brigade duties. Officers Reconnaissance ride of B. Hulls.	cyr
7.12.15.	do. Officers Riding School & Revolver Practice	cyr
8.12.15.	do. Officers Visual training & judging distance exer.	cyr
9.12.15.	do. Officers & available sects. Tactical scheme	cyr
up to 12.12.15	2 men discharged to commissions	cyr
10.12.15.	do. Officers Riding School & Revolver practice	cyr
11.12.15.	do. Foot Root & Kit inspection	cyr
12.12.15.	Church Parade	cyr
13.12.15.	Street fighting. Trench digging, lecture on machine guns	cyr
14.12.15.	Route march and encounter battle	cyr
15.12.15.	Close order drill. Officers Defence of River line	cyr

Army Form C. 2118.

WAR DIARY
INTELLIGENCE SUMMARY.
(Erase heading not required.)

December 1915. O.C. 2/16th London Regt.

Instructions regarding War Diaries and Intelligence Summaries are contained in F. S. Regs., Part II. and the Staff Manual respectively. Title pages will be prepared in manuscript.

Hour, Date, Place	Summary of Events and Information	Remarks and references to Appendices
BISHOPS STORTFORD. 16.12.15.	Ceremonial. Lecture on Trench fighting	cyr
17.12.15.	Inspection of Batt & with transport by OC 179th Infy Bde	cyr
18.12.15.	Kit, Foot & Boot Inspection	cyr
19.12.15.	Church Parade	cyr
20.12.15.	Inspection of Battⁿ by MAJOR GEN E.S. BULFIN CVO CB CB CO 60th London Division.	cyr
21.12.15.	Brigade Duties Coy close order drill.	cyr
22.12.15.	do Officers & Commanders and Defence of a river line & Subalterns visited ONGAR School of Engineering returning same day.	cyr
23.12.15.	Route march. Divisional hot baths opened	cyr
24.12.15.	Foot Rifle Boot & Kit Inspection	cyr
25.12.15.	Church Parade. 2 men discharged to commissions	cyr
26.12.15.	Church Parade	cyr
27.12.15.	Holiday.	cyr

WMcMLachlan
Coy 2/16th London Regt.

WAR DIARY
~~INTELLIGENCE~~ SUMMARY.
(Erase heading not required.)

Army Form C. 2118.

Hour, Date, Place	Summary of Events and Information	Remarks and references to Appendices
28.12.15 BISHOPS STORTFORD	Battalion Concentration March (Coys: to Battⁿ). Average distance 15 miles.	
	Training of selected N.C.O.s & men as Instructors preparating to receiving drafts (350) from 3rd Line, Commenced under the Assistant Adjutant.	
	Lt Col C.A. GORDON CLARK proceeded overseas for temporary attachment to the British Army in the Field. MAJOR F.W.T. ROBINSON, D.S.O. assumed Command of the Battalion. 2nd Lt J LARKWORTHY appointed to commission in 4th Battⁿ South W. York. Reg^t.	AUTHORITY DIV^l ORDER G.396/1.
29.12.15 "	Battalion Close Order Drill. Officers' Reconnaissance.	Y.C.y
30.12.15 "	Attack on a village. —	Y.C.y
31.12.15 "	Brigade duties. Company training. Officers' Revolver practice.	Y.C.y

F.W.T. Robinson Major
Commanding 2/6th Battⁿ xxx Regt

Army Form C. 2118.

WAR DIARY
INTELLIGENCE SUMMARY

2/10TH BATTALION LONDON REGIMENT,
(QUEEN'S WESTMINSTER RIFLES.)

(Erase heading not required.)

Instructions regarding War Diaries and Intelligence Summaries are contained in F.S. Regs., Part II. and the Staff Manual respectively. Title pages will be prepared in manuscript.

Hour, Date, Place	Summary of Events and Information	Remarks and references to Appendices
1916		
Feby 1st LONGBRIDGE DEVERILL	Elementary Training commenced in accordance with Syllabus issued by GO.C 60th Lond. Division. Result of Examination of unclassified members of the Spadding Section received. Was classified as follows :- 1st Class 7; 2nd Class 2; Failed 1.	Syllabus attached Appendix A. W.D.
" 2nd DO	CAPTAIN P.L COCKERILL (informed) attached to H.Q. 179th Brigade returned to duty with his Company. Elementary Training (Contd.). Officers' Transport Drivers Riding School.	W.D.
" 3rd DO	do	
	Route March - 6 miles LONGBRIDGE DEVERILL - PARSONAGE BARN - SHEAR CROSS - LONGBRIDGE DEVERILL - road junction 2 mile S E B (Ref. Ord. Svt. No 122. 1" to mile.)	W.D.
" 4th DO	Elementary Training (Contd.) Riding School 2 Officers Regt. Reinforcement from STAFFORD 144 Other ranks	W.D.
" 5th DO	Physical drill Close order drill Rifle, Kit, Foot & Boot inspections.	W.D.
" 6th DO	Church parades. 5 Recruits received from Dublin	Appendix L.D.377S/A 2/2/16. W.D.
" 7th DO	Elementary Training (Contd.). Riding School. 8 Recruits - taken on Strength 6/2/15 - Inspected by O.C 179th Brigade Capt F. TOWNES Aut Inspector of Q.M.G's services, Southern Command, visited the Camp	W.D.

Army Form C. 2118.

WAR DIARY
INTELLIGENCE SUMMARY
(Erase heading not required.)

2/16TH BATTALION LONDON REGIMENT
(QUEEN'S WESTMINSTER RIFLES.)

Instructions regarding War Diaries and Intelligence Summaries are contained in F.S. Regs., Part II. and the Staff Manual respectively. Title pages will be prepared in manuscript.

Hour, Date, Place		Summary of Events and Information	Remarks and references to Appendices
1916			
February 8th LONGBRIDGE DEVERILL		Elementary training. Capt C.C.G. ROBERTS, Commandant THIRD ARMY TRENCH FIGHTING SCHOOL returned to Battalion for duty	W/S
" 9th " "		Elementary training. One subaltern proceeded to LARKHILL to attend course at Trench Mortar School	W/S
" 10th " "	A.M.	Batt: Route March with Transport. 6 miles	W/S
" " " "	P.M.	Elementary training	W/S
" 11th " "		do. Inoculation IV.	
" 12th " "		Kit, foot, boot & rifle inspection. Physical training. One subaltern + one N.C.O. proceeded to HAYLING ISLAND Watter aquir's Gun Course. One subaltern do do Rifle Course	W/S
" 13th " "		Church parade. Divisional duties	W/S W/S
" 14th " "		Divisional duties. Elementary training. Physical training. Musketry lectures in Camp of Wet weather	W/S
" 15th " "		Elementary training (second week) commenced. Divisional duties. 2nd Lieut F.H. MOORE 2nd ROYAL W SURREY REGT attached 2/Kn.C.R. & 9 men transferred from the 108th Prov Batta to Batta	W/S

(73989) W4141—463. 400,000. 9/14. H.&J.Ld. Forms/C. 2118/10.

Army Form C. 2118.

2/16TH BATTALION LONDON REGIMENT,
(QUEEN'S WESTMINSTER RIFLES.)

WAR DIARY

INTELLIGENCE SUMMARY.

(Erase heading not required.)

Instructions regarding War Diaries and Intelligence Summaries are contained in F.S. Regs., Part II. and the Staff Manual respectively. Title pages will be prepared in manuscript.

Hour, Date, Place	Summary of Events and Information	Remarks and references to Appendices
1916		
February 16th LONGBRIDGE DEVERILL	Divisional duties. Divisional Scheme - postponed owing to inclement weather. Skirmishing Training in camp. 3 NO recruits taken { LT COL GORDON CLARK SICK, CAPT V.C.EGERTON (Honorary) (Command) of ME Battalion } Divisional duties. Divisional Exercise	9/1/g
17th "	2nd Lieut. H. ELSE, KING'S ROYAL RIFLES attached to this Battalion	9/1/g
18th "	Divisional duties. Skirmishing training. Inspection of kit kits. Transport by MAJOR GEN. LANDON, CB. Inspecto Genl. of QM. Services, WAR OFFICE. Musketry Range Practice on open range Commenced	9/1/g
19th "	Bayt, full rifle inspection. Divisional duties.	9/1/g
20th "	Church parade	9/1/g
21st "	Skirmishing training. Musketry Range Practice (Colts).	9/1/g
22nd "	{ Inspection of horses by INSPECTOR of REMOUNT'S, SOUTHERN COMMAND. Lecture to Battalion by CAPT ROBERTS on "Trench construction 9/15 " " " 9/15 }	9/1/g 9/15 9/15
23rd AM "	Route March (with Transport) with Advance Rear Guards	9/15
11.30 am		
PM "	Physical drill. Bayonet work. Lecture to Battalion by CAPT ROBERTS	9/15
24th "	LT COL CA GORDON CLARK returned to duty. Elementary training. Musketry Range Practice (Colts). Inspection of Signallers Lecture by CAPT FLADGATE, 1ST K.R.R. Lecture on Outposts by O.C. Coys.	9/15

Army Form C. 2118.

2/16TH BATTALION LONDON REGIMENT
(QUEEN'S WESTMINSTER RIFLES)

WAR DIARY
or
INTELLIGENCE SUMMARY
(Erase heading not required.)

Instructions regarding War Diaries and Intelligence Summaries are contained in F. S. Regs., Part II. and the Staff Manual respectively. Title pages will be prepared in manuscript.

Hour, Date, Place	Summary of Events and Information	Remarks and references to Appendices
1916 February 25th LONG-BRIDGE DEVERILL	Elementary training. Bayonet fighting course for Officers & NCOs under Lieut. Sergt. BROCKWAY commenced.	
26th "	Bomb, post rifle & rifle inspection. Our Battalion proceeded to HAYING Church parade.	
27th "		
28th "	Elementary training. 5 NCOs commenced course of instruction in Digging under C.R.E., SUTTON VENY	
29th "	Elementary training. 140 N.C.Os & men digging under C.R.E at SUTTON VENY	

[signature]
O.C. 2/16 London Regt.
29.2.16.

Secret

A.G.
3rd Echelon

Herewith War Diary for the month of June 1916.

W Gordon Clark Lt. Col.
Comdg. 2/16th Lond. Regt.

179/60

8.7.16

WAR DIARY OF 2nd BATT~ QUEENS WESTMINSTER RIFLES

INTELLIGENCE SUMMARY

Army Form C. 2118.

(Erase heading not required.)

Instructions regarding War Diaries and Intelligence Summaries are contained in F.S. Regs., Part II. and the Staff Manual respectively. Title pages will be prepared in manuscript.

Hour, Date, Place	Summary of Events and Information	Remarks and references to Appendices
3.30 P.M. June 14th 1915 WARMINSTER	Mobilization Orders received	
" 15th "	Mobilizing and training	
" 16th "	do	
" 17th "	do	
" 18th "	do	
" 19th "	Church Parade & Mobilizing	
" 20th "	do	
" 21st "	do	
" 22nd "	do. 4 Officers attached to Batt~ joined	
" 23rd "	Left WARMINSTER by train to SOUTHAMPTON DOCKS. Marching out state 31 Officers + 973 O.R.	For Officers see Appendix I
" 24th HAVRE	Arrived HAVRE. Batt~ proceeded to DOCKS REST CAMP.	For Strength see Appendix II
" 25th "	Left HAVRE.	" Casualty " " III
" 26th "	Detrained at PETIT HOUVIN. 'A' Coy D Coy + HQ to AVERDOINGT, 'B' Coy 'C' Coy & Sun Subn. to PENIN to billets	" Strength " " IV
" 27th ECOIVRES	Batt~ marched to ECOIVRES to rest camp.	
" 28th "	In rest camp	
" 29th "	do	
" 30th NEUVILLE ST VAAST AREA	Batt~ moved to trenches at NEUVILLE ST VAAST attached to 1/6th BLACK WATCH	
2.30 P.M.	for training. Coys in support & reserve.	
" "	A & B Coy Officers & N.C.Os in front line. One Casualty (wounded)	

W Shorter Captain MC
OC 2/16 London R.

Appendix I
Strength

Date	Details	Strength	
1916 June 21	Attached officers	2/Lt W. MORTIMER (3/7 Mdsx) 2/Lt L.L. FALCK (3/7 Mdsx) 2/Lt F. PAYNE (3/7 Mdsx) 4/Lt N.S. EDMONSTONE (3/7 Mdsx)	9/L ⅝
22	Strength of Batt.	31 Officers 973 O.R. Capt C.M. PHILLIPS & Lt C. SHIPWELL on leave. O.R. 2 Batmen to above officers. " 6 at Divisional H.Q.	9/L ⅝
23	See Casualty Appx	" 1 Off. Strength	9/L ⅝
24	Orderly room Clerk to base	" 1 Off. Strength	9/L ⅝
	March in State	31 officers 971 O.R.	9/L ⅝
30		Officers 33 including Capt Roberts Div. Bombing Officer, Capt Phillips Brigade do. O.R. 965 (13 off Strength to Hospital)	9/L ⅝

London Clark Col.
C.9 2/16 Lond R.

Appendix II

Casualty Return

1916

Date	No	Relate how disposed of	Soldr
June 23	1.O.R	Admd Hospital HAVRE.	
24	1.O.R.	To Hospital	
	1.O.R	To AG's office ROUEN.	
28	1.O.R	To Hospital	
29	3.O.R	To Hospital	
30	1.O.R	To do Wounded - Shell concussion	

Capt J Dunleath Mol
C 7 2/16 2 ond R.

CONFIDENTIAL

WAR DIARY.
OF
2/16 LOND. R.
(QUEEN'S WESTMINSTER RIFLES)

JULY 1916

VOLUME X

WAR DIARY OF 2ND QUEEN'S WESTMINSTER RIFLES

INTELLIGENCE SUMMARY

(Erase heading not required.)

Army Form C. 2118

Instructions regarding War Diaries and Intelligence Summaries are contained in F.S. Regs., Part II. and the Staff Manual respectively. Title Pages will be prepared in manuscript.

Place	Date	Hour	Summary of Events and Information	Remarks and references to Appendices
NEUVILLE ST VAAST AREA	JULY 1st		Trenches. A+B Coys - Platoons in front line for instruction. Attached to 1/5th BLACK WATCH	9/25
"	" 2nd	2pm	C+D Coys relieved A+B Coys. Officers + N.C.Os in front line for instruction. One man wounded.	4/25
"	" 3rd		C+D Coys - Platoons in front line	1/25
"	" 4th		do -- Coys in front line - One man wounded.	4/25
"	" 5th		A Coy H.Q moved to billets at MARŒUIL. B Coy to ABRI CENTRALE. C Coy to ANZIN. D Coy to AUX RITZ CAVES	7/25
MARŒUIL	" 6th		In billets; A Coy HQ. B C + D Coys working parties. (reliefs parties) 2 men wounded. (one died since)	9/25
"	" 7th		do 1 man wounded (died since) A Coy moved to billets at MARŒUIL, C Coy to ABRI	7/25
"	" 8th	8am.	A Coy moved to ANZIN (working parties)	2/25
"	" 9th		CENTRALE; B Coy to ANZIN D Coy +HQ in billets. A Coy at AUXRITZ CAVES, C Coy at ABRI CENTRALE, B Coy at ANZIN (working parties).	2/25
"	" 10th		do do	9/25
"	" 11th		do do	9/25
NEUVILLE ST VAAST AREA	" 12th	11am 2pm	Bomb Sund Section moved to support at MILL STREET - 2 guns, and 2 guns in reserve D Coy moved to VISTULA. A Coy to MONCOP. C Coy to MAISON BLANCHE. B Coy to RHINE, H.Q to RHINE,	4/25 9/25
"	" 13th		do N.I. Support. A Coy - 2 Platoons MONCOP, 2 Platoons to VISTULA, B Coy reserve Centrale, C Coy M2 Subtd.	4/25
"	" 12th	#.30 pm	Bomb gun + section moved to support at M.2 - 2 guns, and 2 guns in reserve at SAPPER SHELTERS	4/25 9/25
"	" 14th		A Coy at VISTULA - 2 Platoons, MONCOP - 2 Platoons, in support, B Coy in reserve Cnte 1, C Coy, M.2.	9/25
"	" 15th		Support. D Coy N.I Support. H.Q at MAISON BLANCHE	9/25
"	" 16th	4pm	Coys moved to firing line Cnte 2 (A B+C Coys) D Coy at ZIVY.	9/25
"	" 16th		A B+C Coys at in firing line Cnte 2. D Coy ZIVY. One man wounded (slight).	9/25
"	" 17th		do do	9/25
"	" 18th		do One man wounded	11/25
"	" 19th		do	11/25
BRAY	" 20th	4pm	A B+C Coys moved to bivouacs at BRAY. D Coy to RHINE SHELTERS. do in Res Hutts at BRAY. D. Coy at RHINE SHELTERS.	11/25

J.B.C. & A. A.D.S.S./Forms/C. 2118.

WAR DIARY of 2ND QUEEN'S WESTMINSTER RIFLES

INTELLIGENCE SUMMARY
(Erase heading not required.)

Army Form C.2118

Place	Date	Hour	Summary of Events and Information	Remarks and references to Appendices
BRAY	July 21st		A.B.&C. Coys at Rest Huts in BRAY. D Coy in Reserve at RHINE SHELTERS. One N.C.O. Killed.	8/15
"	"22nd		do. Physical Drill, Bayonet fighting, Bombing & do. D Coy at RHINE SHELTERS. 3 Captains +	9/15
"	"23rd		Draft of 35 O.R. joined from 3/B Batln. Out. N. Battn. attacked by Chapeau de Gendarmy for instruction, 8 man killed	8/15
"	"24th		do. Route March - 5½ miles	as wounded. 9/15
"	"25th		A.B.&C. Coys at Rest Huts BRAY. D Coy in Reserve at RHINE SHELTERS. One man died of wounds	9/15
"	"26th		do. do.	9/15
"	"27th	6am	Battn: relieved 2/13 Lond. R. in Left Subsector. C Coy on right, D Coy - Centre, B Coy - Left, A Coy -	9/15 9/15
NEUVILLE ST. VAAST AREA	"28th		in Trenches.	9/15 9/15
"	"29th		do. Six men wounded. 2ND LIEUT. L.L. FALCK slightly wounded.	9/15
"	"30th		do. 1 N.C.O. Killed. 1 N.C.O. Died of wounds. 1 man died of wounds. 1 man wounded.	9/15
"	"31st		do. 2 Men wounded.	9/15

M Swainbacher Col.
C 2/16 Lond. R.
Queens Westminster Rifles.
1-8-16

1916

2/16th BATTN. LONDON REGIMENT.
(QUEEN'S WESTMINSTER RIFLES)

STRENGTH

DATE	OFFICERS	OTHER RANKS	
July 1st	31	972	Capt. Phillips, Brigade Bombing Officer, off. Rfm. Rose hospital. 4 A.S.C. attached off strength. Rfm. Jackson Hosp.
	31	971	
" 4th	31	969	Rfm. Given & Kemp hospital
" 6th	31	967	" Best - died of wounds. Rfm. Garrett hospital
	31	966	" E. Thomas hospital
" 7th	31	965	" Sawyer. Killed.
" 12th	31	966	" Given from hospital
" 13th	31	967	" E. Thomas do
" 14th	31	964	" Hymans, Watson & Smithson hospital
	31	952	12 to Trench Mortar Battery. Supernumerary.
	31	943	Rfm. Wright, Peyton, Drew, Sargent, Dennington, Gardner, Jolliffe, Smith N, Peters in hospital
	31	942	Sergt. Payne - Orderly Room Clerk at base.
	31	940	Rfm. Treynier & Given hospital
" 16th	31	936	" Hogg, Parker, Holt, Speck in hospital
" 17th	31	932	" Sander, Thorpe, Conway & Youngman in hospital
" 18th	31	928	" Lee, Gosling, McDowell, Thornton do
" 19th	31	927	L/Cpl Hill in hospital
	31	929	Rfm. Thorpe & Smithson from hospital
" 21st	31	925	" Soar, Hancock, Ingley, in hospital. Corpl. Munday killed
" 22nd	31	923	" Stringer & Tucker in hospital
	31	924	" Speck from hospital
	31	922	" Meager & Miller in hospital
	31	926	Godley, Soar, Holt Gosling from hospital
	31	976	Draft 50 OR from 1/16 Lond R.
" 23rd	31	978	Rfm. Miller & Hogg from hospital
	31	976	Rfm. Paine killed. L/Cpl Elliott wounded
	31	974	" Speck & Everitt in hospital
" 24th	31	978	" Dennington, Hancock, Ingley & Peters from hospital
	31	974	Corpl. Martin, Rfm. Ginger, Boyskell & Pedley in hospital
" 25th	31	975	Rfm. Youngman, Speed, Stringer from hospital. Rfm. Goodman & Pendy to hospital
" 26th	31	969	Rfm. Pollonais killed. Rfm. Mucks, Green, King, Howe, Morley to hospital

2/16 LOND.R.   STRENGTH (Contd).

DATE	OFFICERS	OTHER RANKS	
July 27th	31	968	Rfm. King to Hospital
" 28th	31	966	" Kendall & Greaves to Hospital.
" 29th	31	958	" Ward, Sef & Padbury do. Rfm. de Lara, Onley, Peene, Hele, Whittington & Holder, wounded.
" 30th	31	957	Rfm. Everett, Mackay & Thornton from Hospital. Sergt Kemp killed, Rfm Francis killed. Cpl. Court died of wounds. Rfm Perks wounded.
" 31st	31	948	Rfm Whittington & Holder from hospital. Rfm Skeemer & Foss to hospital. Cpl. Pack, Rfm Willis, Hoffman, Beaumont, Peters, Lording, Duckett, Gaston & Harvey wounded.

W Grant Lieut & OC
C? 2/16 LOND. R.
Queens Westminster Rifles
1-8-16

Army Form C. 2118

WAR DIARY
of 2/16 LOND. R. (QUEEN'S WESTMINSTER RIFLES).
INTELLIGENCE SUMMARY
Part II

Instructions regarding War Diaries and Intelligence Summaries are contained in F.S. Regs., Part II and the Staff Manual respectively. Title Pages will be prepared in manuscript.

(Erase heading not required.)

Vol III

Place	Date	Hour	Summary of Events and Information	Remarks and references to Appendices
NEUVILLE ST VAAST AREA	Aug 1st		In Trenches. Centre 2. C.Coy Right. D.Coy Centre, B.Coy Left. A.Coy in Support at ZIVY. One man wounded	4/15
	" 2nd		do. do. One man killed	4/15
	" 3rd		do. do. Two men wounded.	4/15
	" 4th	8 a.m.	Coys. moved to Support line. A.Coy. N.1. C.Coy MONCOP & VISTULA D.Coy SAPPER SHELTERS, B.Coy in Reserve at RATIONS SHELTERS. HQ at MAISON BLANCHE. Batt. relieved by 1/13 LOND.R.	4/15
	" 5th		Coys in Support line. One man wounded.	4/15
	" 6th		do.	4/15
	" 7th		do. One man wounded. Brought 56 men from L.R.B. and Capt FLOWER att from 3/16 LOND. R. 47 men on strength.	4/15
	" 8th		do.	4/15
	" 9th		do.	1/15
	" 10th		do. Attd: att Demolished.	4/15
	" 11th		do. One man wounded.	4/15
	" 12th	4.30pm	Coys. moved to firing line relieving 2/13 LOND.R. A.Coy on right, C.Coy Centre, D.Coy Left, B.Coy in Support at ZIVY. Work of consolidation of Craters continued. 2nd LIEUT E.B. BROWN in charge of covering party. Out Mine blown at head of SAP 60A at 12.30pm. B.Coy furnished working party to assist in consolidation of crater.	11/15
			One man wounded. (Sapper)	11/15
	" 13		Coys in front line	11/15
			do. One man killed & five wounded	11/15
	" 14th		Coys in front line. Work on consolidation of Craters (contd)	11/15
	" 15th		do. One man wounded	11/15
			do. Following officers joined from 3rd line and taken on strength.— 2nd LIEUTS. S.G. CLAPPEN, R.N. BATES, E.G. CLAYTON, K. FRAZER, & T. WRIGHT.	4/15
	" 16th		Coys. in front line. Work on consolidation continued. Three men wounded. 2nd Lieut WRENN joined from 3rd line taken on strength. One man wounded.	4/15
	" 17th		do. Seven men wounded. (one since died)	4/15
	" 18th		do. Two men killed. One Sergt. wounded (since died) Two Corpls. & six men wounded (one since died)	4/15
	" 19th			
BRAY	" 20th	4 AM	Batt. relieved by 2/13 LOND.R & proceeded to rest billets at BRAY.	4/15
BRAY	" 21st		" in rest camp. Bathing parades.	4/15

Army Form C. 2118

WAR DIARY

INTELLIGENCE SUMMARY

OF THE 2/16th LOND. REGT. QUEEN'S WESTMINSTER RIFLES.

(Erase heading not required.)

Instructions regarding War Diaries and Intelligence Summaries are contained in F. S. Regs., Part II. and the Staff Manual respectively. Title Pages will be prepared in manuscript.

Place	Date	Hour	Summary of Events and Information	Remarks and references to Appendices
BRAY	Aug. 22nd		Battn. in rest huts. Physical drill, bayonet work, rapid wiring practice, bombing practice re	x/25
"	" 23rd		do. Church parade	x/25
"	" 24th		do.	x/25
"	" 25th		do. Route march 4½ miles	y/25
NEUVILLE ST. VAAST AREA	" 26th	2 A.M.	Battn. proceeded to trenches to relieve 2/13 LOND. R. CENTRE 2. B Coy. left; D Coy. centre, A Coy. right; C Coy. support in ZOUY trench. Three men killed. Four men wounded. Two men wounded.	x/25 y/25
"	" 27th		Battn. in front line. One man wounded.	y/25
"	" 28th		do. Three men wounded. Draft of 15 Other Ranks arrived from 3/16th LOND. R.	y/25
"	" 29th		do.	y/25
"	" 30th		do. Two men killed. Six men wounded.	y/25
"	" 31st		do.	

W Shuttleworth Lt. Col.
Comdg. 2/16 LOND. R.

2/16th LONDON REGIMENT
(QUEEN'S WESTMINSTER RIFLES)
— STRENGTH —

1916

DATE	OFFICERS	OTHER RANKS	
August 1st	31	942	Off Strength. To Hospital - Rfm Hurst, Spencer, Smith & Fitzgerald, Lambert (wounded), Lodge (wounded).
" 2nd	31	939	On Strength. From Hospital - Rfm Elliott, Loutson. Off Strength. To Hospital - Rfm Sibbett, Salter, Coney, Longrove, Wallis (wounded).
" 3rd	31	932	Off Strength. Rfm Dadd (killed). To Hospital - Rfm Long, Picker, Fawkes, Morley, Fox, Smith.
" 4th	29	930	Off Strength. 2nd Lieut Edmiston, T.M. Batley seconded. Lt. Falck, wounded 29.7.16. To Hospital - Rfm Lovering, Peachy (wounded), Beale (wounded), L/Cpl Hitchins (Attd 3rd Army Gas School). On Strength From Hospital - Rfm Goodman & Onley.
" 5th	29	927	Off Strength. To Hospital - Rfm Storey, Marsden & Richardson
" 6th	29	929	On Strength. From Hospital - Rfm Peachy, Fawkes, Spencer, Smith. Off Strength. To Hospital. Rfm Burt & Clarke (wounded)
" 7th	30	929	On Strength. Capt Flower from 3/16 LOND. R.
" 8th	30	928 / 927 / 56	On Strength From Hospital. Rfm Onley. Off Strength To Hospital Rfm Ayers & Lowder, Strachan (wounded). Draft from L.R.B.
" 9th	30	927 / 56	Off Strength. To Hospital. Rfm Mitchell. On Strength. From Hospital. Rfm Fox.
" 10th	30	928 / 56	On Strength. From Hospital Rfm Smith, Storey & Hurst. Off Strength. To Hospital. Rfm Speck, Cooper.
" 11th	30	931 / 56	On Strength. From Hospital. Rfm Pedler, Dady, Morley, Richardson, Brown. Off Strength To Hospital. Sergt Jesse, Rfm Brown.
" 12th	30	928 / 56	Off Strength. To Hospital Rfm Hancock, Pedler, Rfm David. On Strength. From Hospital. Rfm Salte.
" 13th	29	921 / 56	On Strength. From Hospital. Rfm Kendall, Longrove. Off Strength. 2nd Lieut E.B. Brown (wounded). Rfm Harper (killed) Rfm Brown, Hipwell, Gordon, Covell, & Morley (wounded) To Hospital Rfm Clement & Duff.
" 14th	29	917 / 56	On Strength. From Hospital. Rfm Lovering. Off Strength. To Hospital. Rfm Thomas, Hancock, Hoff, Fox, Corp. Lucas, Perkins.
" 15th	34	911 / 56	Off Strength. To Hospital Rfm Taylor, Chambers, Bond, Liversley, Clements, Bowles. On Strength. From 3rd Line 2nd Lieuts S.G. Chapman, R.H. Bates, E.G. Clayton, K. Frazer, A.K. Wright.
" 16th	34	913 / 56	Off Strength. To Hospital. Rfm Millard, Wilson. On Strength From Hospital Rfm Gordon, Hymans, Longrove & Packer.

STRENGTH RETURN (Cont'd). 2/16 LOND. R.
(QUEEN'S WESTMINSTER RIFLES).

DATE	OFFICERS	OTHER RANKS	
August 17th	35	910 / 56	Off Strength - To Hospital Rfm Packer & Harkes (wounded) Rfm Miller, Baker & Robinson. On Strength - From Hospital Rfm Hill & Marsden. 2nd Lieut Wrenn from 3rd Line.
" 18th	35	910 / 56	Off Strength - To Hospital. Rfm Abbott. On Strength - From Hospital Rfm Martin.
" 19th	35	898 / 56	Off Strength - Rfm Peet & Banham (killed) To Hospital - wounded. Sergt Groome (died of wounds) Rfm Scruton (died of wounds) Rfm. Palmer, Stewart, Cooper, Filler, Barnard & L/Cpl Guttery. Sick - Rfm. Lewin & Clavey.
" 20th	35	894 / 56	Off Strength - To Hospital Rfm Rowland & Riches (wounded) Rfm Jarvis & Spooner. Under age - Rfm Rogers, Brissenden & Bowles. On Strength - From Hospital - Rfm Pedler, Middleditch & Drew.
" 21st	35	901 / 56	On Strength - From Hospital Rfm Wilson, Lowden, Foss, Kedge, Bond, Walton, Perkins. Off Strength - To Hospital. Rfm Carnan & Hawkes.
" 22nd	35	901 / 56	On Strength - From Hospital - Rfm Mitchell & Corp.
" 23rd	35	903 / 56	On Strength - From Hospital - Rfm Beale & Gardner.
" 24th	35	929 / 56	On Strength - From Hospital - 26 OR Rfm Smith & Hawkes, Tucker, Argyle & King. Off Strength - To Hospital - Rfm Lambert.
" 25th	35	933 / 56	On Strength - From Hospital. Rfm Dicken.
" 26th	35	934 / 56	On Strength - From Hospital - Rfm Stewart.
" 27th	35	931 / 56	Off Strength - To Hospital Rfm Taylor & Bond. Rfm Ansell (Gwm) to 179th Brigade.
" 28th	35	928 / 56	Off Strength - To Hospital. Rfm Ellis, Entwistle, Carlinger, Abbott, Lowden. On Strength - From Hospital Rfm Palmer & Barnard.
" 29th	35	928 / 56 / 15	Draft of 15 Other Ranks from 3/11th LOND. REGT arrived.
" 30th	35	926 / 56 / 15	Off Strength - To Hospital Rfm Choulton (wounded) Rfm Carnan & Mitchell. On Strength - From Hospital Rfm Lowden.
" 31st	35	919 / 56 / 15	Off Strength - To Hospital Rfm Cumms, Clinging, Staples, Smith N.C. Hugh. Killed - Rfm A. Payne & L.S. Smith.

(Sa Sutherland) Lt Col
Cmdg 2/16 LOND. REGT

1.9.16.

CONFIDENTIAL.

WAR DIARY.

OF THE

2/16TH BATTALION LONDON REGT.
(QUEEN'S WESTMINSTER RIFLES).

SEPTEMBER 1ST TO 30TH 1916.

VOLUME IX.

Army Form C. 2118

WAR DIARY of 2/16 LOND. R.

INTELLIGENCE SUMMARY QUEEN'S WESTMINSTER RIFLES.

(Erase heading not required.)

Instructions regarding War Diaries and Intelligence Summaries are contained in F.S. Regs., Part II. and the Staff Manual respectively. Title Pages will be prepared in manuscript.

Place	Date	Hour	Summary of Events and Information	Remarks and references to Appendices
NEUVILLE ST VAAST AREA	Sept 1st	4.30am	Battn. relieved by 2/13 LOND. R. returned to Support. A Coy SAPPER SHELTERS, D. Coy BENTATA, B Coy - 2 platoons MONCOP, 2 platoons - VISTULA, C Coy RHINE. H.Q. MAISON BLANCHE. Two men wounded.	9/1
"	" 2nd		Coys in Support - Casualties 1 + 2. One man wounded.	9/2
"	" 3rd		do	9/3
"	" 4th		do	9/4
"	" 5th		do	9/5
"	" 6th		One man wounded.	9/6
"	" 7th	6-10 am	Battn. moved to front line. CENTRE 2 & relieved 2/13 LOND. R. B Coy Left; C Coy Centre, A Coy Right - D Coy in Support at ZIVY. B Coy 2/11 LOND. 2 platoons MONCOP - 2 platoons VISTULA. A Coy 2/11 LOND. RHINE & ELBE. One of our mines blown by us in PHILIP GROUP of CRATERS at 3.15 pm. 2nd LIEUTS. C.H. BANNATT & C.C. WALL joined from 3rd line and taken on strength.	9/7
"	" 8th		Coy in front line. One man killed. One man died of wounds. 1 NCO & 6 men wounded.	9/8
"	" 9th		do. Five men wounded.	9/9
"	" 10th		do. One man killed. Two men wounded.	9/10
"	" 11th		do. One man killed.	9/11
"	" 12th		do. Five men wounded.	9/12
BRAY	" 13th	8-10 AM	Battn. march to NEUVILLE & BRAY. The following Officers joined from 3rd line & taken on strength - 2nd Lieuts F.D. Relieved by 3/13 LOND. R. MASSON, A.M. ALEXANDER, B. GARLICK, J.H. YOUNG.	9/13
"	" 14th		Batn in Rest Huts. Baths. General Salute to	9/14
"	" 15th		do Brigadier Bulfin. Bathing or Divisional Digging Parties. Lieutenant B DENT joined from	9/15
"	" 16th		Batn Luts to ?? ?? Strength. Ant Res in Rest Huts. ?? Bath, Bathing or Divisional Digging Parties.	9/16
"	" 17th		do. Church Parade 6.30 pm	9/17
"	" 18th		do. Brays of 20 OR joined from 3rd line & taken on strength.	9/18
NEUVILLE ST VAAST AREA	" 19th	8 PM	Battn. relieved 3/13 LOND. R. in front line. CENTRE 2. B Coy Left, D Coy Centre, C Coy Right, A Coy Support at ZIVY. One man killed. Six men wounded.	9/19

1875 Wt. W593/826 1,000,000 4/15 J.B.C. & A. A.D.S.S./Forms/C. 2118.

WAR DIARY of the 2/16th BATTALION LONDON REGT.
INTELLIGENCE SUMMARY (QUEEN'S WESTMINSTER RIFLES).

Army Form C. 2118

Instructions regarding War Diaries and Intelligence Summaries are contained in F. S. Regs., Part II. and the Staff Manual respectively. Title Pages will be prepared in manuscript.

(Erase heading not required.)

Place	Date	Hour	Summary of Events and Information	Remarks and references to Appendices
NEUVILLE ST VAAST AREA	Feb. 20th		Coys. in front line. One man killed. 2nd Lieut G.M. DOLBY displayed courage & contempt for danger under fire in carrying round of heat chocolate. Who were served by T.M. Shapcombe.	W/S 2/2
"	" 21st		do. One man killed.	2/2
"	" 22nd		do. One man wounded.	2/3 Operation Orders No. 20 and Report Appendix II 2/2
"	" 23rd		do. A successful raid on enemy trenches was carried out at 11pm. One man missing. Eight NCOs & men wounded.	
"	" 24th		do.	
"	" 25th	6-10 AM	Battn. relieved by 2/3 LOND. R. & moved to support line. A Coy. RUINE. B Coy. No 2. C Coy. K.I, D Coy. MONCOP & FISTULA. 2nd Lieut. ELCHAYER joined from 3rd Army reinforcement strength. Recommendations for honours forwarded in connection with Raid on the 23rd Sept:—	See Appendices III
"	" 26th		Coys. in Support line. LIEUT. C.S. MIPNELL for Distinguished Service Order 2ND LIEUT. W. MORTIMER for Military Cross 3750 L/CORPL. W.E. KNOX for Military Medal 3387 CORPL. J. ARCHER 5403 RFM. F.W. BARNES 5110 " C.F. STOREY 3491 CORPL. T. HARDING 2340 / SERGT. N.M. MANSELL 3336 SERGT. T.H. SMITH	
"	" 27th		Coys. in support line. One man wounded.	2/2
"	" 28th		do. CAPT.C.O SPENCER SMITH joined from 3rd line & taken on strength.	2/2
"	" 29th		do.	W/2/2
"	" 30th		do.	2/2

W Jackson Clark Major
C? 2/16 LOND. R.
Queens Westminster Rifles.

To H.Q., 179 Inf Bde.

FURTHER REPORT on RAID carried out by 2/16 LOND.R. on 23.9.16.

In continuation of my previous report dated 24.9.16 I have the honour to state that Capt.T.H.FLOWER deserves the greatest credit for the exact arrangements which he carried out under my orders and the careful training which he conducted at HERMAVILLE and in the trenches, the results of which are shown in the strict discipline with which the raid was carried out.

I wish to draw attention to the conduct of Lieut.C.S. HIPWELL who by his thoughtful and very gallant leading minimised our losses and stimulated all ranks to display their courage and discipline. He and 2nd Lieut.W.MORTIMER after the raid was over went out a second time to search for Rfn. WATERMAN who was wounded in the first journey across NO MAN'S LAND. After a very thorough search, in which they were aided by Lieut.F.C.HIPWELL and 2nd Lieut.A.ARCHIBOLD, the search had to be given up. The body of this rifleman has since been discovered in NO MAN'S LAND close to the German wire to the left of the routes followed.

I wish also to draw attention to the gallant conduct of:-

(1) 2nd Lieut.W.MORTIMER, who went from point to point of the fighting in the trenches seeing that all were in their proper places, encouraging them and waited to count them out of the trenches at the conclusion of the raid. He also as stated above went out again under continuous fire to search for a wounded man.

(2) No.3336 Sergt.T.H.SMITH whose cool conduct and bearing was of of the utmost value. This N.C.O. has previously done very good patrol work round the new crater in the PHILLIP group, which lies almost on the enemy's firing line.

(3) No.2340 Sergt.W.M.MANSELL who remained with his party in the enemy's wire making the road home easy, and xxxixx passing prisoners across, under fire nearly all the time.

(4) No.3750 L/Corpl.W.E.KNOX (wounded) who held off the enemy in a lively fight with his bombing squad and captured prisoners, refusing help when offered.

(5) No.3357 Corpl.J.ARCHER who led his bombing squad and captured a N.C.O. and private himself by a well conceived ruse, before commencing to bomb the enemy in the communication trench.

(6) No.3491 Corpl.T.HARDING who posted his bombing party before the biggest number of the enemy and then himself captured two prisoners and killed or wounded at least four men.

(7) No.5453 Rfn.F.W.BARNES who defended his wounded comrade and had a blanket thrown over his head, but managed to get rid of it and bayonet his assailant, being slightly wounded in both hands.

(8) No.5110 Rfn.C.F.STOREY who as front bayonet man with many Germans in front of him, was wounded, but bayonetted his assailant and kept away the remainder whilst Corpl.HARDING TOOK HIS PRISONERS from a dug out.

I attach statement of officers and sergeants.

In conclusion I think I am right in xxxixx stating that the whole party enjoyed their raid immensely.

24.9.16.

STATEMENTS by Officers and N.C.O's
————————————————————

24.9.16.

Lieut.C.S.HIPWELL states

At 9 p.m. I went out nearly as far as enemy wire and located gap, and returned. I heard working on my right and believed I heard a patrol or covering party getting out on my right. I got back at 10.15 p.m. Rfn. Cable and Clark accompanied me.

At 10.45 p.m. the raiding party started from point of concentration, and proceeded to point of exit and crawled out between 70 and 80 yards, this bringing us within about 30 yards of enemy wire. We reached this point at 10.59 p.m. At this time firing was opened upon us from a covering party on our right taking us in my right flank, Very soon after this a machine gun opened upon us from the left, fired about 25 shots when a loud explosion was heard and its fire ceased.

At 11 p.m. the Howitzer barrage opened, followed almost immediately afterwards by the Stokes. At this moment the leading party ran forward and fire was opened from a bay immediately behind the gap in the wire. In consequence of this we bore slightly to the left and tackled a piece of uncut wire about 3 feet high where it was less thick than in other places. One blanket was dropped and I got over the wire with its aid, climbed the parapet, and was fired at at close range by 5 or 6 rifles. I replied with my revolver and they ceased fire. I then returned to the wire and helped to lay further blankets. The whole party then crossed in correct order and all went direct to their places. The first party in was timed at 11.3 p.m. I remained with one ladder man standing on the parapet, where I obtained a good view and helped prisoners over it.

The parties were all in by 11.6.p.m. After 5 prisoners had been handed up and sent back under escort I gave the word for Return at just about 11.10 p.m. All were out by 11.12 p.m, and returned by the same route, Sgt.Mansell & his party having been xxxxxxxxxxxxxxxxxxxxxxxxxxxxxxxxxxxxxxxxxxxxxxxx engaged in cutting more wire and relaying blanket bridges, and continuing the tapes as far as the enemy parapet. All parties except one reported correct as they came up the ladder; the party which failed to report was the KNOX party, the reason being that Corpl. Knox was badly wounded as he came out. 2nd Lieut. Mortimer and Sergt. Smith consequently ran back to search but found no more men, and the KNOX party having been checked by Sergt. Mansell at the wire, I ordered these two to return. I then returned. By 11.15 p.m. I had reached our wire and the signal to return was heard and seen at that moment. On returning we picked up the casualties which had occurred on our way out with the exception of Rfn. Waterman who fell early in the advance.

Every party did the exact work for which it was told off and came out in their proper order.

The prisoners all used the ladders but the men of party climbed over by the fire step.

There was no hesitation at any time on the part of any man and it is exceedingly difficult to single out any who did better work than another. 2nd Lieut. Mortimer was very cool and collected and gave invaluable help in seeing that all were in their proper places and kept to the programme. Sergt. Smith behaved exactly as though on parade. Corpl. Archer's party was extremely well handled. Corpl. Harding took two prisoners and

(2)

killed or wounded at least four Germans. Rfn. Storey was first in the trench and was wounded as front bayonet man, but carried on in the face of a crowd of Germans. Rfn. Barnes killed his man after having had a blanket thrown over his head; he was wounded in the hand. Rfn. Burton, who was wounded in the thigh and arm, tackled a number of Germans from among whom two prisoners were taken. It was this group of Germans who showed most fight.

Corpl. Archer was for a time alone in the communication trench and took 1 N.C.O. and 1 man prisoner before his party started throwing bombs in return

2nd Lieut. W. MORTIMER states

I followed out at the head of the raiding party. Rfn. Waterman was in my party behind me and I did not see him wounded. We waited until the Artillery opened about 40 yards outside point of exit; whilst waiting the enemy was firing at the party. I counted seven rifles; they might have been just in front of their wire. On arriving at the point of entry we lay down until wire bridges were in position. I got in touch with the left and centre blocking parties, found them in their right places and assisted to bring down their prisoners. I found no dug out in communication trench, but I did in the firing line. Before leaving a P bomb was put into this dug out by Sergt. Smith.

After seeing all out of the trench, Sergt. Smith and I rejoined Lieut. Hipwell and went back, leaving Lieut. Hipwell to come last. The tapes made a high road from parapet to parapet and were brought in later. Sergt. Mansell did very good work in cutting wire, laying tapes, and marshalling prisoners over NO MAN'S LAND.

I could not see what Lieut. Hipwell did before I got to him; he remained on the parapet to the last and carried back the ladder until it got firmly fixed in wire.

Sergt. Smith's coolness and presence of mind in keeping bombers supplied, passing back prisoners, helping men over the parapet and generally seeing that everyone who needed help obtained it, was admirable.

No. 3336 Sergt. T.H. SMITH states

On going out I was with the rear party, and Rfn. Waterman just in front of me was shot I think in the thigh. I said as I passed - "Stick it, we shall soon be back". None of the other men left the line when they passed him. On arrival in the trenches, I visited the bombing parties on left and centre; both reported all right and that they could hold them. I helped to pass the prisoners along and when word was passed to go back I passed it to the blocking parties; and when these had passed out I put a P bomb into a dug out shaft which fizzed but did not appear to go off. I accompanied Lieut. Mortimer back. The officers stuck there until they were quite sure that no one remained before returning.

The men did their work in such a manner that there was no need for any direction by the N.C.O's. The corporals of the blocking parties led their men with a grand spirit of leadership and fought well.

Sergt. Mansell on the covering party did very well to make the road smooth for the remainder; he was under fire nearly all the time.

No.2340 Sergt.W.M.MANSELL states

Lieut. Hipwell and I cut the wire on our side the night previously. He went out to reconnoitre and came back; then our party started and we picked up as we went out all the articles which I had previously laid out. After going some distance we were fired on by from 8 to 12 rifles on our right. I thought we had little chance of success as the parapet appeared to be manned, but as the first How. fired Lieut.Hipwell ran on. I followed him and placed my blanket on the wire. Lieut.Hipwell at once jumped on it and from it into the wire, and thence on to the parapet where he stood up and was fired at. He replied with his revolver. I shouted for the other blanket men and they laid them out as we had practised; they then took up their allotted positions. For half a minute Lieut. Hipwell was there by himself whilst we were putting on the blankets and cutting the wire. Then the stream came along; they did not shout but ran in their order quickly across the bridge and flopped into the trenches. I could find no gap in the wire so commenced cutting. The next was a call for ladders; these were passed through. I then found one of my ladder men was a casualty. As we were getting the tapes up to the parapet the first prisoner was handed over, then three more. I sent them on and one got stuck in the wire. I had to use ½ inch of bayonet to make him jump clear of the wire, and tell off an escort from my party. When all the parties except the officers and Sergt. Smith had passed a few moments elapsed, and I got the word from Lieut.Hipwell Home. We could not get the bridges off the barbed wire and all walked home. If we had gone for the gap which was cut we should not have got in, as the parapet was lined with rifles there.

Lieut.Hipwell's dash forward and standing on the parapet with his revolver in his hand was what gave such a lead to all of us that we could do nothing wrong.

COPY OF LETTER RECEIVED FROM G.O.C. 1st. ARMY.

G.O.C. XVIIth CORPS.

I should be glad if you will ask the G.O.C. 60th Div. to convey to Brigadier General Baird, Comdg. 179th. Infy. Bde. my appreciation of the successful raid carried out last night by the 2/6th LONDON REGT. under Lt.Col.C.A.Gordon Clark.

The gallantry and initiative displayed by all ranks taking part in the raid, and the careful preparations made beforehand, led to a most successful operation, including the capture of prisoners, which at the present time is most important for purposes of identifications.

(Signed) R. HAKING, General.
24th Sept. 1916.   Comdg. 1st. ARMY.

COPY OF LETTER RECEIVED FROM H.Q. XVII CORPS.

60th. DIVISION.

The Army Corps Commander wishes me to say that he has read this report with great interest and considers that it reflects the utmost credit on all concerned.

The appreciation of the Army Commander will be gratifying to all ranks.

(Signed) J.R.E. CHARLES,
25th. Sept. 1916.   Brigadier-General.

Extract from Battn Routine Orders dated 25th Sept. 1916.

1. "THE RAID OF 23rd. SEPT.

The Commanding Officer has received very flattering congratulations from the G.O.C. 1st Army, G.O.C. XVII Corps, G.O.C. 60th Division and the G.O.C. 179th. Infantry Brigade.

The G.O.C. 1st. Army sent an autograph letter, the other three made personal visits. The G.O.C. XVII Corps said that it was a model of what a raid should be for the purpose for which it was ordered, and that it proved not only the valour but the extremely good discipline of the battalion.

The Commanding Officer is very happy and thanks Capt. Flower for all the arrangements and the training, Lieut. C.S. Hipwell for his determination, skilful and gallant leadership and all ranks of the raiding party for the gallant conduct and successful fighting powers.

Unusually valuable information has been obtained."

EXTRACT FROM DIVISIONAL ROUTINE ORDERS

1014. HONOURS AND REWARDS.

Under authority granted by His Majesty The King, the Army Corps Commander has awarded the following decorations for gallant conduct on the 23rd. September 1916.

2/16th (County of London) Battalion. The London Regiment. (Queen's Westminster Rifles) (T.F.).

No.3357 Corporal JOHN ARCHER - Military Medal

Date of Award. 29th September, 1916.

Led a bombing party with great courage, coolness, and resource during a successful raid on the enemy trenches on 23rd. September 1916. He captured single-handed a German N.C.O. and Man, and then held off the remainder of a hostile party with his bombing squad, acting as front bayonet man, and inflicting substantial losses on them.

No.5750 L/Cpl. WILLIAM EDWARD KNOX - Military Medal.

Date of Award, 29th September, 1916.

Led a bombing party with great skill during a successful raid on the enemy trenches on 23rd. September 1916. He held off the enemy in a lively fight with his bombing squad and captured two prisoners, refusing help when offered. He was severely wounded when seeing the last of his squad out of the hostile trenches.

No.5463 Rfn. FREDERICK WILLIAM BARNES - Military Medal

Date of Award, 29th September 1916.

During a successful raid on the enemy Trenches on 23rd September 1916, he ran to the assistance of a wounded man who was surrounded by Germans. A blanket was thrown over his head but, although wounded in both hands, he succeeded in getting rid of it and bayonetted his assailant, driving back the rest of the party.

Appendix II

EXTRACT FROM DIVISIONAL ORDERS.

1043. HONOURS AND REWARDS

Under authority granted by His Majesty The King, the General Officer Commanding-in-Chief has awarded the following decorations for gallant conduct on the 23rd. September 1916.

2/16th (County of London) Battalion. The London Regiment. (Queen's Westminster Rifles). (T.F.).

Lieut. CHARLES STANLEY HIPWELL. - Military Cross.

Date of Award. 3rd October 1916.

Lieut. Hipwell led a successful raid into the enemy trenches on the 23rd. September 1916 which resulted in the capture of prisoners. He engaged a fire bay full of Germans and silenced them with his revolver, remaining standing on the parapet while his men crossed the hostile wire, and thereafter until the last man had left for our lines.

He went out again under continuous fire to search "No Man's Land" for a wounded man.

The success of the raid was due to his determination and resourceful leading.

1078. HONOURS AND REWARDS

Under authority granted by His Majesty The King, the General Officer Commanding-in-Chief has awarded the following decoration for gallant conduct on the 21st September 1916.

2/16th (County of London) Battalion. The London Regiment. (Queen's Westminster Rifles) (T.F.).

2nd.Lieut. GEOFFREY NORMAN DOLBY - Military Cross.

Date of Award. 10th October 1916.

On the 21st September 1916, 2nd.Lieut.Dolby went to the assistance of three wounded men whose post was destroyed by a Trench Mortar, although these men were not under his command. He remained with them throughout an accurate Trench Mortar bombardment, was twice knocked over by the explosions, extricated two of the injured from the debris, would not allow other helpers into the danger zone, and finally got all three wounded men to the Aid Post

REPORT ON RAID CARRIED OUT IN ACCORDANCE WITH MY

OPERATION ORDERS NO. 20 dated 21. 9. 1916.

1. The Raid was successfully accomplished at 11 p.m. on 23.9.16. The Raiders left the PULPIT CRATER SAP at 10.55 and were all back in our Trenches by 11.30 with the exception of one wounded man.

2. Five prisoners were taken belonging to the 104th Regiment XIX Saxon Corps. 1 N.C.O. and 4 men, one of the latter being wounded in the head by a club. The number of German casualties in addition is estimated at from 14 to 20.

3. Our casualties were two men seriously wounded, 4 slightly wounded. 1 wounded and missing.

4. On starting the Raiding Party came under steady Rifle Fire from a covering party in front of Enemy wire some 50 yards to our Right. This was the cause of most of the casualties. The Officer in command however judging that this Covering party would come under our barrage fire as soon as it started waited for the signal and then held on for his objective. The Trench was found to be full of Germans and contained several Dug-outs.
The Trenches were of chalk, 8½ feet deep, very narrow with narrow fire step and in bad condition, only occasional pieces of revetment being seen: No duck-boards, traverses very broad, parados very high indeed.

5. The Enemy with one or two exceptions ran away rather than fight, certain men used their Rifles well but none accepted close fighting.

6. All the arrangements made were rigidly adhered to and answered their purpose well.

7. The Howitzers fire was most accurate, the Stokes barrage was well carried out and was seen to cause a casualty to a Rifleman standing up on the parapet.
The 2" T.M. of Y60 which had been asked to fire on a certain emplacement opposite LICHFIELD CRATER silenced the Machine Gun with its first shot after it had fired 25 shots.
The Enemy's T.M. replied and he also fired some half dozen 77 on our Support Line, presumably at the decoy lights.

8. The Medical arrangements worked well; from the Aid Post in Line to Advanced Dressing Station was a straight run.

9. After the Raid, Officers Patrol went out and searched the whole of NO MAN'S LAND for a wide stretch for the man who fell wounded between the tapes on going out and must have crawled away before the return of the Raiding Party. Every yard was gone over under a Rifle Fire and when near enough to hostile lines, sharp Bomb Showers. Lights were also thrown along the ground which burst into two red balls.

10. The careful attention to all details given by Captain C.H.FLOWER contributed greatly to the success of the Raid.
The very skilful leading and resourceful bravery of Lieut. S. HIPWELL was undoubtedly the cause of the success of the Raid. He was ably seconded by 2/Lieut. W. MORTIMER. All the N.C.Os. and men behaved exceedingly well and in every case are reported to have carried out the duties allotted to each with accuracy and joyful alacrity.
I wish to collect further details of individual actions, and report further. Meanwhile I hope that Lieut. S. HIPWELL and 2/Lieut. W. MORTIMER may be considered for special mention.

- 2 -

11. A further report will be prepared after receipt of written reports from the Officers engaged.

(sd) C.A. GORDON CLARK,
Lieut-Col.
24th September 1916.   Comdg. 2/16th LONDON REGT.

The following CODE will be used by Capt Flower.
MARE and HORSE.

Raiding Party gone out.   PROCEED
    "   "   held up.   PLAY.
    "   "   in enemy trenches.   ENJOY.
    "   "   returning.   REPLACE.
    "   "   all in   SATISFIED.
    "   "   all in except)   REGRET.
Our killed   )   CUBE
Our wounded   ) Followed   TICKLE
Our missing   )   DALLY
Prisoners captured   ) by No.   SPOIL
Enemy killed   )   HASTACE

The following pass words will be used by Raiding Party as Countersign.

         " QUEENS "   " HALL "

The word to be used when party moves to exit and comes home will be:-

         " LAMP BLACK "

SCHEDULE "A".

Detail of Parties with Duties and Equipment.

1. **Covering Party (MANSELL PARTY).**
    O.C.: Lieut. S. Hipwell, and 1 Runner,
    1 N.C.O. and 8.
    Duties: <u>To cover advance</u>, and remain on Enemy parapet.
        To clear wire.
        To lay blanket bridges.
        To carry ladders.
        To lay tapes.

    10 Rifles and swords, 20 bomb carriers small, 40 Mills, 9 wire cutters hand, 10 wire cutters rifle, 9 gloves, 4 ladders, 3 blanket bridges, 1 club, 2 tapes, bombing shields, 9 rounds in mag. 1 in chamber, 1 revolver.

2. **Right Blocking Party (HARDING PARTY).**
    1 N.C.O. and 5.
    Duties: To block Fire Trench 25 yards South of Point of Entry, and remain till O.C. orders return. 1 N.C.O. and 1 man deal with dug out if met with.

    4 Rifles and swords, 6 Bomb carriers small, 3 Bomb Carriers large, 42 Mills bombs, 4 wire cutters rifle, 2 clubs, bombing shields, 9 rounds in mag., 1 in chamber.

3. **Left Blocking Party (KNOX PARTY).**
    1 N.C.O. and 4.
    Duties: To block fire trench 10 yards North of BALLOON AVENUE and return as soon as centre blocking party has passed them after completion of raid; this is on hearing the word "last man of ARCHER party".

    4 Rifles and swords, 6 bomb carriers small, 2 bomb carriers large, 32 Mills Bombs, 4 wire cutters rifle, 1 club, bombing shields, 9 rounds in mag., 1 in chamber.

4. **Centre Blocking Party (ARCHER PARTY)**
    1 N.C.O. and 4.
    Duties: To block BALLOON AVENUE 30 yards East of Fire Trench, and return on word from O.C. MORTIMER party.

    4 Rifles and swords, 6 bomb carriers small, 2 bomb carriers large, 32 Mills bombs, 4 wire cutters rifle, 1 club, bombing shields, 9 rounds in mag., 1 in chamber.

5. **First Raiding Party (MORTIMER PARTY).**
    1 Officer and 7.
    Duties: To raid BALLOON AVENUE and Dug-outs within 18 yards of Fire Trench, and return on word from SMITH party.

    7 Rifles and swords, 14 bomb carriers small, 1 bomb carrier large, 32 Mills Bombs, 7 wire cutters rifle, 8 clubs, 2 P bombs, bombing shields, 9 rounds in mag., 1 in chamber, 1 revolver.

6. **No. 2 Raiding Party (SMITH PARTY).**
    1 N.C.O. and 4.
    Duties: To lay tapes.
        To raid Fire Trench between point of entry and BALLOON AVENUE and return on receiving word from O.C. Raid, which

C A G C

Start from Concentration point
X — 15

If prisoners captured, return as early as possible without waiting for Bugle or Rocket.

(a) Telephone to R.A. direct or to me if guns are to stop before X + 20.

(b) Send runner to M.G. to stop fire & dismiss

(c) Send runner to Sr Giannacopulo to stop rockets being sent up.

(d) Inform me at once

If wounded direct to stretcher bearers dug out. If more than one, then second & third to MINE SHAFT.

All these orders are to be handed in before leaving Centre Coy Dug out.

W&S

- 2 -

word is passed to MORTIMER Party.

5 Rifles and Swords, 8 bomb carriers small, 1 bomb carrier large, 20 Mills bombs, 5 wire cutters rifle, 5 clubs, 2 bombs P, bombing shields, 9 rounds in mag., 1 in chamber, 2 tapes.

Total Strength: LIEUT. S. HIPWELL.
                   2ndLieut. W. MORTIMER.
                   38 O.R.

NOTES: Each man carries Field Dressing in trouser pocket.
       Chocolate and biscuit and water in lower tunic pockets.
       2 clips of ammunition in breast pockets.
       White chalk circles at corners of skirt of bombing shields.

       Leaders of parties carry Electric Torch and Magnetic Compass.

                                 (sd) C.A.GORDON CLARK.
                                       Lieut-Col.
                               Comdg. 2/16th London R.

S E C R E T.
Copy No.

OPERATION ORDERS NO. 20
by
Lieut-Colonel C. A. GORDON-CLARK,
Comdg. 2/16th London Regiment (Q.W.R.)
....
21st September 1916.

Ref: NEUVILLE Squared Map.

1. A party of 2 Officers and 38 O.R. commanded by Lieut. B. HIPWELL, will carry out a raid on the German Trenches between A.4.d.37.06 and A.4.d.40.26 on the night of 23.9.16

2. The object is the capture of prisoners and documents and to inflict loss on the enemy.

3. Captain C.H. FLOWER will carry out all the arrangements here detailed.

4. The 2" T.M's will cut wire along our Front on 20th, 21st and 22nd September and at A.4.d.37.13 on 23rd.
The Lewis Guns will keep the gaps in the wire open. The Field How. Battery on 22nd and 23rd September has been ordered to bombard T.M. positions at A.4.b.60.10.

note 18 lbs did not fire.

5. On the night of 23.9.16 at X *(11.pm)* the 18 lbs. and Field How. Batteries will bombard the following points for 20 minutes:
    A.10.b.35.76.
    A.10.b.60.95.
    A. 4.d.65.16 and
    From A.4.d.45.58 to A.4.d.66.46.
The Stokes Gun will bombard A.10.b.36.77 and one Machine Gun will fire from SAP 43b. on to A.10.b.37.95.
Lewis Guns will fire on selected points of our Line.

6. The point of departure for the raid will be the old post in SAP 43d leading to Right Post of PULPIT CRATER.
The point of Concentration will be two Dug-outs at the Centre Coys. H.Q.

X-15 = 10.45 pm

7. The raiders will start from Concentration point at X-15 and from point of departure at X-5 min. in the order and with dress and duties in accordance with Schedule A. *(10.55 pm)*
The point of entry to German Lines will be A.4.d.37.13.

8. The raiders will return to point of departure leaving point of entry at X+ 15 minutes, and will all proceed direct to the point of concentration, where the roll will be called and N.C.O. in charge of each party will report all present or otherwise to CAPTAIN FLOWER. *(11.15 pm)*

9. A telephone wire will be laid from Centre Co.H.Q. to Central Group R.A., for Code see Schedule B.

10. At X+5 four lamps will be shown in Support Line near ZIVY REDOUBT. *(11.5 pm)*
O.C. Right Co. will send up flares at X+2
At X+2 a feint bombardment will be ordered on the Left of our Front *(11.2 pm)*
At X+15 the signal for retirement will be given; (i) bugle call "COOKHOUSE"; (ii) A white rocket sent up at Junction of GUILLERMOT and THELUS Road by Lieut. GIANNACOPULO and repeated every 30 seconds until X+18. *(11-15 pm)*

11. Tapes will be laid by the leading and the Rear Files of the Raiding Party from point of departure to point of entry

12. The whole party will get as near hostile Trenches as possible before X when Artillery opens. On Artillery opening the party will at once rush the allotted Trenches. *(11.pm)*

OPERATION ORDERS NO. 20 (contd.)

13. Prisoners will be disarmed and taken to point of entry and handed over to O.C. party who will send them to point of concentration.

14. Casualties will be ignored until the retirement is carried out, and then every effort will be made to bring all back.
4 Stretcher Bearers and 2 Runners from D. Coy. and 1 Bugler will be posted in SAP 43d.

15. Watches will be synchronised at a time and place to be notified later.

16. No documents, badges or Battalion Titles will be carried. Faces will be blacked, bayonets dulled.

17. The proper conduct of prisoners of War will be explained to all Ranks taking part.

18. The garrison of No. 2 Sub-Sector will be under cover except the Sentries, from X until bombardment on both sides ceases. Schedules A and B attached. (Schedule B (Code) will be forwarded later).

19. Captain FLOWER will report to Bn. H.Q. at frequent intervals.

(sd) C.A. GORDON CLARK.
Lt.Col.
Issued at
Comdg. 2/16th LONDON R.

No. 1 Copy: War Diary.
2 " H.Q., 179th Inf.Bde.
3 " Capt. FLOWER.
4 " O.C., "A" Coy.
5 " O.C., "B" Coy.
6 " O.C., "C" Coy.
7 " O.C., "D" Coy.
8 " O.C., Stokes Guns.
9 " O.C. Machine Gun Coy.

Scale abt. 1/5000

SKETCH showing
2/16ᵗʰ OPERATION ORDER
dated 21 July 16

SAXON'S
BREAST

EDINBURGH

A point of departure
B point of entry
C Right Block
D Left Block
E Centre Block
F Machine Gun
G point of concentration

21·9·16

1a Somewhere ?
C.J.G. WR

2/16th BATT. LONDON REGIMENT
(QUEEN'S WESTMINSTER RIFLES).

STRENGTH.

DATE	OFFICERS	OTHER RANKS	
1916			
Septr. 1st	35	989	
" 2nd	35	989	
" 3rd	35	990	On Strength. Fr Hospital 4. Off Strength. To Hospital 3.
" 4th	35	990	
" 5th	35	990	
" 6th	35	989	Off Strength To Hospital 1.
" 7th	35	991	On Strength. Fr Hosp. 3. Off Strength To Hosp. 1.
" 8th	35	988	Off Strength To Hosp. 3.
" 9th	37	991	On Strength - 2 Officers (2nd LIEUTS. C.H. DANNATT & C.C. HALL) do - Fr Hospital 5. Off Strength. To Hosp. 2.
" 10th	37	989	Off Strength - To Hosp. 2.
" 11th	37	993	On Strength. Fr Hosp. 4. Off Strength - 1 man killed in action
" 12th	37	984	Off Strength. 1 man killed in action. To Hosp. 8.
" 13th	37	983	do - 1 man killed in action.
" 14th	41	981	On Strength - 4 Officers (2nd LIEUTS. MASON, A.M. ALEXANDER, G. GARLICK, J.H. YOUNG) Fr Hosp 3. Off Strength To Hosp. 5.
" 15th	41	979	On Strength. Fr Hosp 1. Off St. To Hosp. 3.
" 16th	42	976	On Str. 1 Off (2nd LIEUT H.B. DENT). Off Str. 1 man died of wounds. To Hosp. 2.
" 17th	42	968	On Str. Fr Hosp 1. Off Str. To Hosp. 4.
" 18th	42	984	On Str. Draft of 20. O.R. Off Str. 1 man died of wounds. To Hosp. 2. 1 man to Havre for dentures.
" 19th	42	987	On Str. Fr Hosp 5. Off Str. To Hosp 2.
" 20th	42	987	—
" 21st	42	986	Off Str. 1 man killed in action
" 22nd	42	986	Off Str. 1 man died of wounds. On Str. Rfmn A King Struck off in error 31.8/16.
" 23rd	42	983	Off Str. 1 man died of wounds, 1 man killed in action, 1 man med. unft. To Hosp 1. On Str. Fr. Hosp 1.
" 24th	42	978	Off Str. To Hosp 5.
" 25th	42	976	Off Str. 1 man died of wounds. To Hosp 3. On Str. Fr Hosp 2.

STRENGTH.   APPENDIX I (Cont.)

1/17th BATTN: LOND REGT.

DATE	OFFICERS	OTHER RANKS	
Sept. 26th	42	979	On Strength. Draft of 7 O.R. joined from 3/16th Battn. Lond. R. Off Str. To Hosp: 4.
" 27th	43	972	On Strength. 1 Off (2nd E.C.TAYLOR). Off Str. To Hosp 7.
" 28th	43	973	On Str. To Hosp 3. Off Str. To Hosp 2.
" 29th	43	968	Off Str. 1 man missing. 4 men tos. to Machine Gun Coy.
" 30th	44	963	Off Str: 2 men tos to M.G. Coy, 1 to Trench Mortar Battery, 1 to Corps Intelligence Police, 1 to Commission, 1 to Hosp. On Strength. Reinforcements 1 Off. (CAPT. C.O. SPENCER SMITH) + 1 O.R.

Vol 5

Secret

WAR DIARY
of
2/16th Batt London Regiment
from
1st October 1916 to 31st October 1916

WAR DIARY

12/15th LOND. REGT. (QUEEN'S WESTMINSTER RIFLES)

Army Form C.2118

INTELLIGENCE SUMMARY
(Erase heading not required.)

Instructions regarding War Diaries and Intelligence Summaries are contained in F.S. Regs., Part II. and the Staff Manual respectively. Title Pages will be prepared in manuscript.

Place	Date	Hour	Summary of Events and Information	Remarks and references to Appendices
NEUVILLE ST VAAST AREA	Oct 1st	5-9 p.m.	Battn. relieved 2/13th LOND. R. in front line. D Coy Left, C Coy Centre, A Coy Right, B Coy Support ZIVY. D Coy 2/14 RHINE	V/S 1
"	" 2nd		Supports MONCOP & VISTULA. B Coy 2/14 RHINE. Coys in front line CENTRE 2. One man wounded.	V/S 2
"	" 3rd		do Four men wounded. 2nd LIEUT M.M. MART joined from 3rd Line station on strength.	V/S 3
"	" 4th		do Lt. Col. C.A. GORDON CLARK assumed command of the 179th Infantry Brigade at the Battalion	V/S 4
"	" 5th		do MAJOR V.C. EGERTON Two men killed & one wounded. Award of Military Cross to 2/Lieut. C.S. HIGNELL	V/S 5 See appendix II
"	" 6th		Cpl. enfront line CENTRE 2. One man wounded.	V/S 6
"	" 7th		Battn relieved by 2/13 LOND.R moved to rest huts at BRAY	V/S 7
BRAY	" 8th		Another an rest huts. Cleaning up equipment & clothes. Baths. Church parade.	V/S 8
"	" 9th		do Church parade. Baths. Physical Drill, Bayonet work. Class rifle drill.	V/S 9
"	" 10th		do Trench fighting. Battn & Coy class rifle drill.	V/S 10
"	" 11th	9.30 am	Battn. inspected by Lt. General Sir CHARLES FERGUSSON Bt, K.C.B, M.V.O, D.S.O. commanding XVII Corps. Parade late 31 Officers 645 OR. (Returns of R. Artillery given. Whilst paraded to audit disposed & 2nd Lt F.W. BARNES regd ahead of supposed cross to 2nd Lt G.N. DOLBY dimissed. 1 P.M. Small fighting in trenches dept.)	V/S 11
"	" 12th		Battn. in rest huts. Physical drill & bayonet work. P.M. All Coys. Anti Aircraft Ruterment drill.	V/S 12
NEUVILLE ST VAAST AREA	" 13th	3AM	Battn. left BRAY to relieve 2/13 LOND R in front line. B Coy A/c, D Coy Centre, A Coy Right, C Coy Right Support ZIVY.	V/S 13
"	" 14th		Coy 2/13 Support at MONCOP & VISTULA. Coy 2/14 Support at RHINE. Two men wounded	V/S 14
"	" 15th		Coys in front line. LIEUT. C.S. HIGNELL R.C. Killed in Action. One man killed. One man died of wounds. Two men wounded. 2nd LIEUT. F.R. LEETH & Father to through H.	V/S 15
"	" 16th		do Two men killed. Two men wounded.	V/S 16
"	" 17th		do Four men wounded. Lt. Col. C.A. GORDON CLARK wounded. Lt. Col. GORDON CLARK wounded on leave. MAJOR V.C. EGERTON assumed command A Coy MONCOP & VISTULA. B Coy BENZATA, Coy SAPPER	V/S 17
"	" 18th		do Four men wounded.	V/S 18
"	" 19th	4.30-8 am	Battn. relieved by 2/13 LOND. R. transferred to Support line. A Coy MONCOP & VISTULA, B Coy BENZATA, Coy SAPPER, D Coy RHINE.	V/S 19

Army Form C.

WAR DIARY ⅟₂/16th LOND. REGT.

INTELLIGENCE SUMMARY (QUEEN'S WESTMINSTER RIFLES).

(Erase heading not required.)

Instructions regarding War Diaries and Intelligence
Summaries are contained in F. S. Regs., Part II.
and the Staff Manual respectively. Title Pages
will be prepared in manuscript.

Place	Date	Hour	Summary of Events and Information	Remarks and references to Appendices
NEUVILLE ST. VAAST AREA	Oct. 20th		Companies in Support line. Two men wounded.	W.S.
"	" 21st		do	W.S.
"	" 22nd		One man killed. Two men wounded. H.Q. Staff 60th Battn: CANADIAN INFANTRY visited MAISON BLANCHE for instructions for relief of Battn: on the 24th inst.	W.S.
"	" 23rd		Companies in Support Line. O.C. Coys. 60th Battn: CANADIAN INFANTRY visited respective numbers in this Battn: in Support line for instruction.	W.S. W.S.
"	" 24th	8pm	Companies in Support Line. Battn: relieved by 60th Battn: CANADIAN INFANTRY. marched to rest huts at BRAY. (6¾ miles)	W.S.
BRAY	" 25th	2pm	Battn: marched to TILLOY-HERMAVILLE. L 179th Anspots Machine Gun Coy. attached to the Battn; Lt. Col. C.A. GORDON CLARK resumed command of the Battn:	W.S.
TILLOY-HERMAVILLE	" 26th		Left TILLOY-HERMAVILLE 9am. arrived SIBBEVILLE 3.20pm. 12¾ miles.	W.S.
SIBBEVILLE	" 27th		Battn: in SIBBEVILLE.	W.S.
SIBBEVILLE	" 28th		do left SIBBEVILLE 9.30am. att VILLERS L'HOPITAL 8 miles	W.S.
VILLERS L'HOPITAL	" 29th		do left VILLERS L'HOPITAL 8am. arr: RIBEAUCOURT 1.40pm. A & D Coys billeted at DOMESMONT. 11¾ miles. 13 miles.	W.S.
RIBEAUCOURT & DOMESMONT	" 30th		do in RIBEAUCOURT & DOMESMONT. Coy training	W.S.
"	" 31st		do do do	W.S.

[signature]
17 ⅟₆ Lond R
Queens Westminster Rifles

H.Q.   Appendix 111
60th Div. 20-10-16.

The following remarks by the Corps Commander on his his inspection of the 2/16th LOND.R. have been received.

" Good in all respects. The men were smart, clean and well turned out. They were perfectly steady under arms, and stood well in the ranks. The condition of the battalion was most creditable."

To. O/C 2/16th Battn, London Regt.

The Birgadier congratulates you on the report made on your Battn, after the Corps Commanders inspection, and feels sure that your Battn, will always keep up the reputation, which it has earned.

H.Q. 179th INF.BDE. 20-10-16.

2/16th Battn. London Regt
(QUEEN'S WESTMINSTER RIFLES)
DAILY STRENGTH RETURN.

DATE	OFFICERS	OTHER RANKS	
October 1st	44	966	
" 2nd	44	964	2 Men tis. to H.Q. 179th Brigade (Supernumerary)
" 3rd	45	961	3 " admitted to Hospl. 2nd LIEUT K. HART joined.
" 4th	45	961	1 " " " " 1 Man rejoined from Hospl.
" 5th	45	961	
" 6th	45	957	2 Men killed in Action. 2 Men admitted to Hospl.
" 7th	45	954	1 Man rejoined from Hospl. 4 Men admitted to Hospl.
" 8th	45	955	" " "
" 9th	45	955	2 Men admitted to Hospl. 1 Man rejoined from Hospl. 1 man joined Irish Divn.
" 10th	45	956	1 Man rejoined from Hospl.
" 11th	45	953	2 Men admitted to Hospl. 1 Man to Commission.
" 12th	45	953	1 Man rejoined from Hospl. do.
" 13th	45	952	1 Man admitted to Hospl.
" 14th	45	949	4 Men admitted to Hospl. 1 Man rejoined from Hospital
" 15th	46	953	2ND LIEUT F. B. LEETE joined (Reinforcement) 2 men joined (reinforcement) 3 Men rejoined from Hospl. 1 Man admitted to Hospital.
" 16th	45	951	LIEUT. C.S. HIPWELL Killed in action. 1 Man Killed in action 1 Man admitted to Hospital.
" 17th	45	985	Draft g 37. O.R taken on strength. 2 Men killed in action. 1 man died of wounds.
" 18th	45	981	4 Men admitted to Hospital.
" 19th	45	977	1 Man killed in action. 3 Men admitted to Hospital.
" 20th	45	978	1 Man rejoined from Hospital.
" 21st	45	974	3 Men admitted to Hospl. 1 N.C.O. to Commission
" 22nd	44	971	2nd LIEUT GARLICK to England Sick. 4 men admitted to Hospll. 1 man fr. Hospll.
" 23rd	44	971	
" 24th	44	971	
" 25th	44	971	
" 26th	44	971	
" 27th	44	972	1 Man Killed in action. 4 Men admitted to Hospll. 6 men returned from Hospital
" 28th	44	972	
" 29th	44	972	
" 30th	44	976	4 Men rejoined from Hospital.
" 31st	44	975	1 Man admitted to Hospital

CONFIDENTIAL.

WAR DIARY
OF
2/16 BATTN. LONDON REGT.
(QUEEN'S WESTMINSTER RIFLES)

NOVEMBER 1ST TO 30TH 1916.

VOLUME XII

WAR DIARY
of 2/16th Battⁿ LONDON REGT (QUEEN'S WESTMINSTER RIFLES)
INTELLIGENCE SUMMARY

Army Form C.2118

(Erase heading not required.)

Instructions regarding War Diaries and Intelligence Summaries are contained in F.S. Regs., Part II. and the Staff Manual respectively. Title Pages will be prepared in manuscript.

Place	Date	Hour	Summary of Events and Information	Remarks and references to Appendices
RIBEAUCOURT & DOMESMONT	Nov 1st/16		Battn. in RIBEAUCOURT & DOMESMONT. Coy. training. 2nd Battn. inspected in RIBEAUCOURT - BEAUMETZ road by the Commander-in-Chief (GENL SIR DOUGLAS HAIG, K.C.B., K.C.M.G., etc.)	W.S.
"	" 2nd		do. do. Coy. training	W.S.
"	" 3rd	9.55am	Battn. marched to BELLANCOURT (14 miles)	W.S.
BELLANCOURT	" 4th		Battn. in BELLANCOURT. Coy. training. Orders received that Battn. would shortly be proceeding overseas.	W.S.
"	" 5th		Battn. in BELLANCOURT. Church Parade. made up to strength of 35 Offrs + 580 O.R. Transport in accordance with War Estab. Part XII	W.S.
"	" 6th		do Coy. training	W.S.
"	" 7th		do do	W.S.
"	" 8th		do do	W.S.
"	" 9th		do do	W.S.
"	" 10th		do Brigade. Major E.W. BEARD bade farewell to the Battn. on relinquishing his command of the 179th Infantry Brigade.	W.S.
"	" 11th		do do	W.S.
"	" 12th		at Church Parade. Tactical scheme. Lt. Col. in Command + Coy. Commanders attended Brigade scheme held by J.M. EDWARDS D.S.O. G.O.C. 179th Infantry Brigade	W.S.
"	" 13th		do Route march 8½ miles	W.S.
"	" 14th		do	W.S.
"	" 15th		Battn. entrained at LONGPRÉ for MARSEILLES	W.S.
"	" 16th		En route for MARSEILLES	W.S.
EN ROUTE FOR MARSEILLES	" 17th	12.20 am	Left MARSEILLES + marched to CARCASSONNE Camp.	W.S.
MARSEILLES	" 18th		Battn. in MARSEILLES	W.S.
"	" 19th	11am	Embarked on H.M.T. TRANSYLVANIA 36 Offs. 883 O.R. Left Quay at 10pm	W.S.
AT SEA	" 20th		At Sea	W.S.
"	" 21st		do	W.S.
MALTA	" 22nd	10am	Battn. arrived at MALTA. Officers only allowed on Shore (Valetta) 10ff, 20 OR + 23 horses mules embarked on H.M.T. MENOMINEE etc.	W.S.
"	" 23rd		At MALTA. Left for VALETTA. Officers only allowed on shore.	W.S.
"	" 24th		do do	W.S.
"	" 25th		do do Sailed from MARSEILLES	W.S.
"	" 26th		do	W.S.

WAR DIARY

OF 2ND BATTN. LOND. REGT.

INTELLIGENCE SUMMARY (QUEEN'S WESTMINSTER RIFLES).

Army Form C. 2118

Place	Date	Hour	Summary of Events and Information	Remarks and references to Appendices
MALTA	Nov 27th	10.30am	H.M.T. TRANSYLVANIA left MALTA	
AT SEA	" 28th		Battn. at Sea.	
"	" 29th		do	
SALONIKA	" 30th	10.15am	Battn. arrived at SALONIKA. Disembarked marched to Rest Camp (6 mile) arr. 5pm	

W. Sutherland Mol
O.C. 2/16 Lond R.

2/1 BATT'N LONDON REGT
(QUEEN'S WESTMINSTER RIFLES)

STRENGTH.

DATE	OFFICERS	OTHER RANKS	
1916.			
Nov'r 1st	44	975	
" 2nd	44	975	
" 3rd	44	974	1 N.C.O. transferred to R.E.
" 4th	44	974	
" 5th	44	971	1 Man tr's: (under age) 2 Rfm. admitted to Hospital.
" 6th	44	945	28 Men admitted to Hosp'l 1 Rfm tr's. to R.F.C. 3 Rfm fr Hosp'l
" 7th	44	945	1 Rfm tr's (under age) 1 N.CO from Brigade (supernumerary).
" 8th	44	945	
" 9th	44	945	1 N.C.O + 2 Rfm admitted to Hosp'l. 1 N.C.O + 2 Rfm discharged fr. Hosp'l.
" 10th	44	946	1 Man discharged fr. Hosp'l.
" 11th	44	948	1 Rfm fr F.R.C. 3 Rfm discharged fr. Hosp'l 1 N.C.O tr's. unfit 1 Rfm. tr's. to Div'l H.Q.
" 12th	44	951	3 Rfm. discharged from Hosp'l.
" 13th	44	950	1 Rfm. discharged fr. Hosp'l.
" 14th	44	950	
" 15th	44	933	7 N.C.Os + Rfm admitted to Hosp'l 1 N.C.O + 8 Rfm tr's to
" 16th	44	933	Machine gun coy. 1 Rfm tr's to Base (unfit).
" 17th	44	933	
" 18th	38	904	6 Officers (CAPT SPENCER SMITH, CAPT BARCLAY 2nd LIEUTS CLAPPEN, HALL, YOUNG, DENT) + 25 N.C.Os + Rfm struck off strength to complete new Establishment. 1 N.C.O discharged to Commission 1 N.C.O on leave tr's. to Base. 3 Rfm under age tr's to Base.
" 19th	38	906	O.R. Clerk tr's from Base. 1 Rfm discharged from Hosp'l
" 20th	38	903	1 N.C.O discharged to Commission.
" 21st to 29th	38	905	—
" 30th	38	905	—

60 DIVISION

179 INF BRIGADE

2/16 LONDON REGT
(QUEENS WESTMINSTER RIFLES)

1915 SEP — 1916 FEB

2902

www.ingramcontent.com/pod-product-compliance
Lightning Source LLC
Chambersburg PA
CBHW081452160426
43193CB00013B/2455